SPOTLIGHT ON PHYSICAL SCIENCE

MOTION

EXAMINING INTERACTIONS

DANIEL R. FAUST

PowerKiDS press

NEW YORK

Published in 2020 by The Rosen Publishing Group, Inc.
29 East 21st Street, New York, NY 10010

Editor: Elizabeth Krajnik
Book Design: Michael Flynn

Photo Credits: Cover, p. 1 Denis Belitsky/Shutterstock.com; (series molecular background) pro500/Shutterstock.com; p. 4 Jacek Chabraszewski/Shutterstock.com; p. 5 Wallenrock/Shutterstock.com; p. 6 Photo 12/Universal Images Group/Getty Images; p. 7 https://commons.wikimedia.org/wiki/File:NewtonsPrincipia.jpg; p. 9 Izf/Shutterstock.com; p. 10 Bplanet/Shutterstock.com; p. 11 MaszaS/Shutterstock.com; p. 12 Andrey Yurlov/Shutterstock.com; p. 13 bondvit/Shutterstock.com; p. 14 junpinzon/Shutterstock.com; p. 15 Nomad_Soul/Shutterstock.com; p. 17 Antonio Gravante/Shutterstock.com; p. 18 Hogan Imaging/Shutterstock.com; p. 19 Ian Thraves Photography/Shutterstock.com; p. 20 Andrey Armyagov/Shutterstock.com; p. 21 courtesy of NASA; p. 22 Farid Suhaimi/Shutterstock.com; p. 23 BlueRingMedia/Shutterstock.com; p. 25 Soule' Photography/Shutterstock.com; p. 26 Tommy Alven/Shutterstock.com; p. 27 Yicai/Shutterstock.com; p. 29 Jeff Kowalsky/Bloomberg/Getty Images; p. 30 Suzanne Tucker/Shutterstock.com.

Cataloging-in-Publication Data

Names: Faust, Daniel R.
Title: Motion: examining interactions / Daniel R. Faust.
Description: New York : PowerKids Press, 2020. | Series: Spotlight on physical science | Includes glossary and index.
Identifiers: ISBN 9781725313293(pbk.) | ISBN 9781725313323(library bound) | ISBN 9781725313309(6 pack)
Subjects: LCSH: Motion--Juvenile literature. | Kinematics--Juvenile literature. | Force and energy--Juvenile literature.
Classification: LCC QC133.5 F375 2020 | DDC 531'.11--dc23

Manufactured in the United States of America

CPSIA Compliance Information: Batch #CWPK20. For further information contact Rosen Publishing, New York, New York at 1-800-237-9932.

CONTENTS

CHAPTER ONE

WHAT IS MOTION?

You get up and ride your bike to school. You open a drawer to look for a pencil. You toss a ball to your friend. What do all these things have in common? They're all examples of motion. Motion is the action of changing an object's location or position. Motion can result in a change of location, such as when you go from home to school. Some motion is **repetitive** and **fluctuates** between two positions, like opening and closing a drawer. Rotation, or spinning, is another kind of motion.

Everything in the universe moves, even if we can't see it happening. Some things move very slowly and travel great distances while other things only move small distances. For example, Earth rotates on its axis constantly, but you can't feel it. You also can't feel Earth orbiting the sun.

Once you realize that motion is everywhere, you'll start to see how motion is a part of almost everything we do.

CHAPTER TWO

NEWTON'S LAWS

Much of what we know about motion can be traced back to the work of Sir Isaac Newton. Newton was a 17th-century English astronomer, mathematician, and **physicist**. Newton was also a natural philosopher, or someone who studied nature and the physical world in the days before modern science. Many of Newton's laws and **theories** helped form the basis of our understanding of the universe.

SIR ISAAC NEWTON

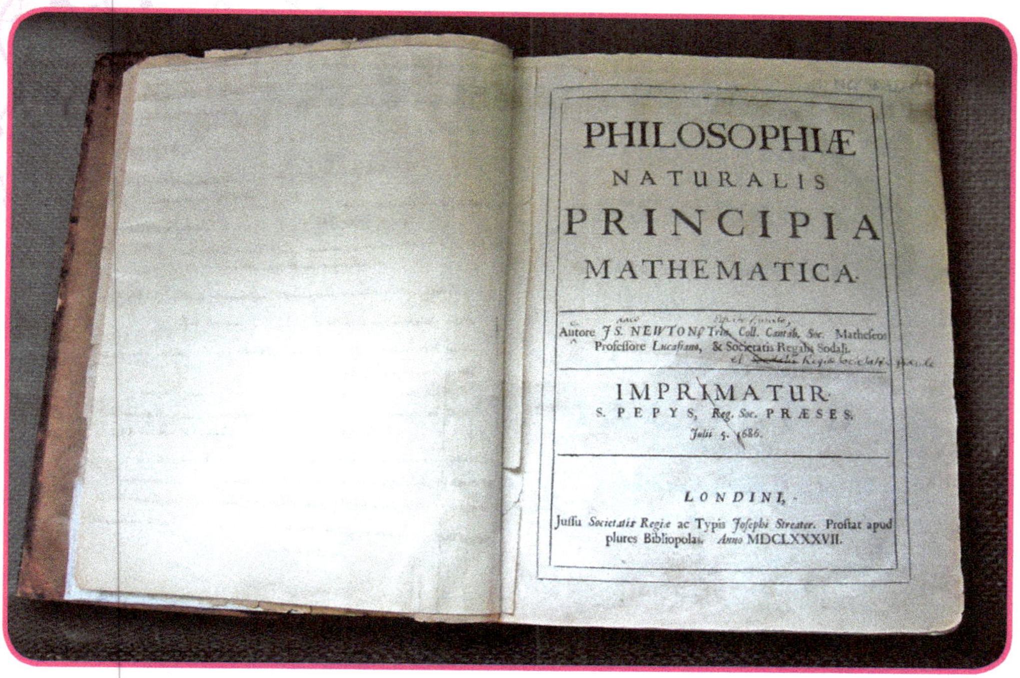

PHILOSOPHIÆ
NATURALIS
PRINCIPIA
MATHEMATICA.

Autore J S. NEWTONO, Trin. Coll. Cantab. Soc. Matheseos Professore *Lucasiano*, & Societatis Regalis Sodali.

IMPRIMATUR.
S. PEPYS, *Reg. Soc.* PRÆSES.
Julii 5. 1686.

LONDINI,

Jussu *Societatis Regiæ* ac Typis *Josephi Streater*. Prostat apud plures Bibliopolas. *Anno* MDCLXXXVII.

Even though it was published in 1687, Newton's *Principia* is still considered one of the most important works of modern science.

Many people know the story of how Newton watched an apple falling from a tree, which led to him theorizing that a force had acted upon the apple. Newton's observation led to his law of gravitation, which helped explain planetary motion and the interaction between celestial bodies such as planets and moons. In 1687, Newton published his theory of gravitation, along with his three laws of motion, in *Philosophiae Naturalis Principia Mathematica*, or simply *Principia*.

CHAPTER THREE

INERTIA AND FRICTION

According to Newton's first law of motion, an object at rest (or one moving in a straight line at a constant speed) will keep doing so unless an outside force acts upon it. That means that if a ball is sitting still on a flat surface, it will remain still unless something pushes it. If it's moving in a specific direction at a specific speed, it will continue to move in that direction and at that speed unless it encounters an outside force.

The **tendency** for an object to stay at rest or remain in motion is called inertia. All matter has inertia. An object's inertia can only be changed if an outside force acts upon the object. Gravity is one of the forces that can change an object's motion. Another force is friction. Friction is the **resistance** to motion caused when one object rubs against another.

The wheels of a skateboard rub against the ground as it moves forward. This causes friction and, along with gravity, causes the skateboard to slow down.

CHAPTER FOUR

THE FIRST LAW OF MOTION IN ACTION

What does Newton's first law of motion look like in action? Imagine you kick a ball along the floor. The ball was at rest until you kicked it. Your kick is the force. Now that the ball is moving, inertia will keep the ball in motion until another force acts upon it. Maybe the ball hits the wall and stops. Maybe a friend kicks the ball in another direction.

If you took the ball outside and kicked it up into the air, what do you think would happen? Two forces would act on the ball's inertia: gravity and friction. The ball would only be able to go so high before the force of Earth's gravity would pull it back toward the ground. And even though you can't see it, the ball is rubbing against the **molecules** in the air, creating friction that slows it down too.

Most people don't realize the role that physics plays in everyday activities such as sports. When basketball players pass the ball or shoot a basket, they have to take gravity and friction into consideration.

CHAPTER FIVE

ACCELERATION AND MASS

Newton's second law of motion states that the **acceleration** of an object is directly related to the magnitude, or strength, of the force applied to it. The law also says that the object will move in the direction of the force applied and that the acceleration will be inversely related to the mass of the object. This means that the greater the mass, the less the acceleration.

When someone says a car can go from 0 to 60 miles (0 to 96.6 km) per hour in a certain amount of time, they're talking about how quickly the car can accelerate. Miles per hour and kilometers per hour are units that measure acceleration.

Mass is a measurement of how much material is in an object. For example, a baseball has less mass than a car. Newton's second law says that if you apply the same amount of force to two objects of different mass, the objects will accelerate at different rates. The object with the smaller mass will have a greater acceleration than the object with greater mass.

CHAPTER SIX

THE SECOND LAW OF MOTION IN ACTION

It's easy to push an empty shopping cart, isn't it? An empty shopping cart has little mass, so it doesn't take a lot of force to move it. If you load up that shopping cart with things for your family, you increase your burden's mass. Now it'll take more force to move the shopping cart. Without extra force, a full shopping cart will not move as quickly as an empty shopping cart.

Now, let's say you and a friend each have your own empty shopping cart and you want to race. Since you know Newton's second law of motion, you know that both carts will accelerate at the same rate if similar amounts of force are applied. Because you want to win the race, you'll have to apply more force to your cart to make it accelerate quicker than your friend's cart.

Cars have a lot of mass, much more mass than an empty or full shopping cart. It takes a lot of force to push a car even a short distance because its mass is so great.

CHAPTER SEVEN

EQUAL AND OPPOSITE

Motion can't exist without force. In physics, force is what is known as a vector quality. This means that force has both direction and magnitude. If you apply a force to an object in order to move it, you have to apply that force in a specific direction.

According to Newton's third law of motion, every action has an equal and opposite reaction. This means that whenever two objects interact, they **exert** forces on each other. Forces are always found in pairs. The magnitude of the force acting on the first object is equal to the magnitude of the force acting on the second object. However, the direction of the force acting on the first object is opposite to the direction of the force acting on the second object.

If you blow up a balloon and let it go, it will fly around the room. This is because the air is being pushed out of the balloon, which causes the balloon to be pushed forward. This is one example of Newton's third law of motion in action.

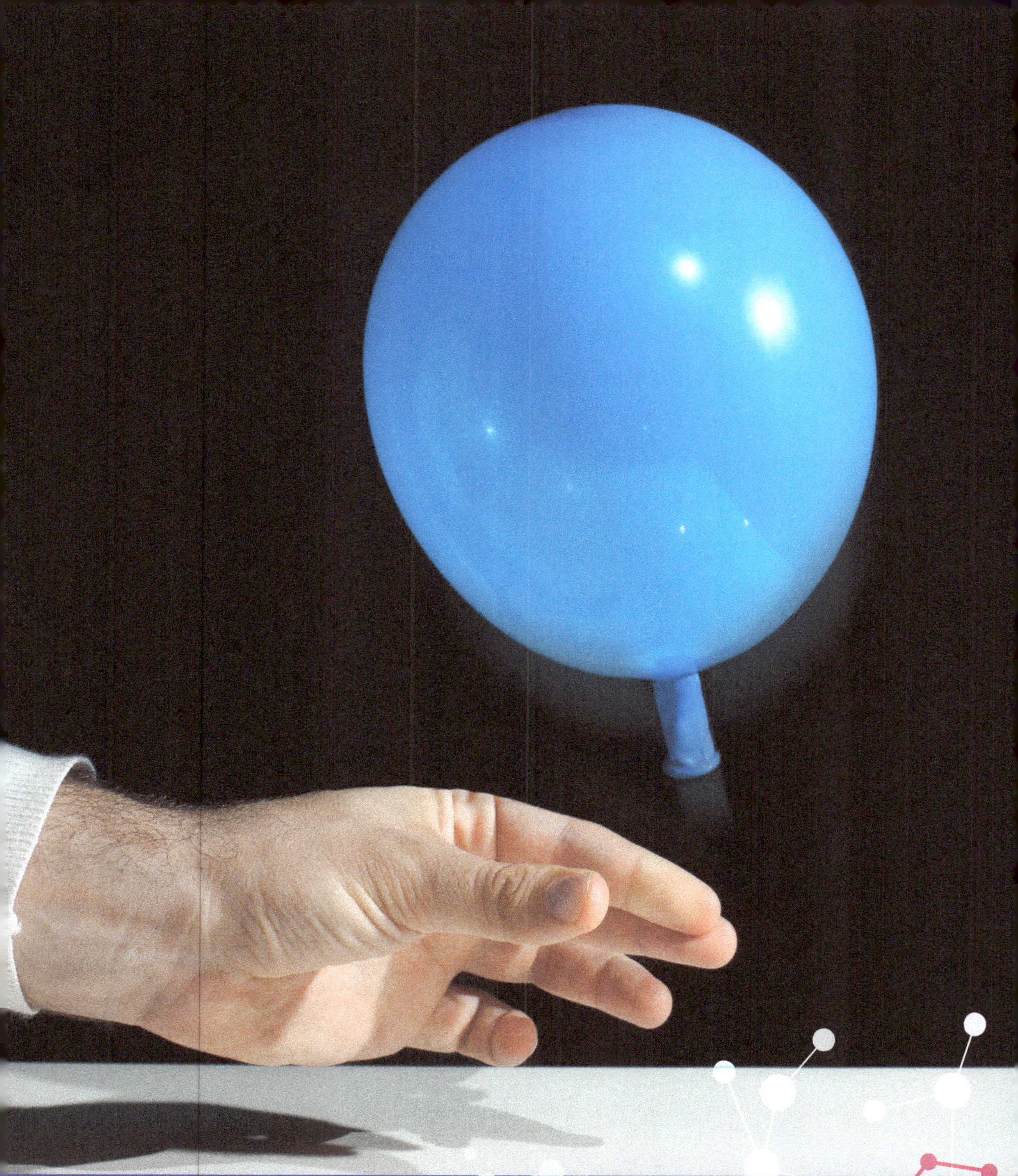

CHAPTER EIGHT

THE THIRD LAW OF MOTION IN ACTION

When you sit down on a chair, your body exerts a downward force on the chair. The chair exerts an equal upward force on you. If the chair didn't push back on your body with an equal force, it would collapse. The interaction between your body and the chair is an example of Newton's third law of motion in action.

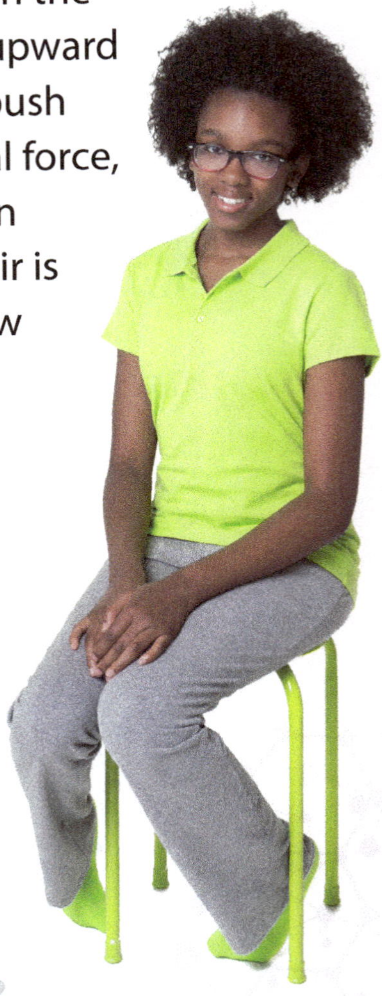

Another example of Newton's third law in action is when a cannon fires. When the cannon fires, the force of the exploding gunpowder shoots the cannonball forward, but an equal force from the cannonball pushes back on the cannon.

Newton's third law also explains how airplanes fly. Planes fly by balancing four equal and opposite forces. Thrust, which is the force the plane's engine or propeller creates, pushes the plane forward. Air pushes back against the plane, creating drag. As the plane moves forward, air is forced over the plane's curved wings. Lift is created when the wings force this air down, pushing the plane up. In order to get off the ground, a plane must generate enough lift to counteract the plane's weight.

CHAPTER NINE

MOTION IN SPACE

Everything in the universe is in motion, including the planets, moons, and stars. Planets orbit a star because of the tug-of-war between the star's gravitational force and the planet's inertia. This is called centripetal force. Centripetal force is also what keeps **satellites** in orbit around Earth.

Astronauts in Earth orbit experience microgravity, which is a condition in which people or objects appear to be weightless. Microgravity occurs because the astronauts and their spacecraft are falling toward but around Earth at the same rate. The astronauts and the objects around them appear to be weightless because they're in free fall.

When an agency such as NASA launches a rocket into space, they're using Newton's third law of motion. The rocket generates a downward force that pushes against the ground to create lift. Scientists and engineers needed to figure out how fast a rocket had to go in order to break free of Earth's gravity. This speed is known as escape **velocity**. A rocket needs to be going about 25,000 miles (40,234 km) per hour to escape Earth's gravitational force.

CHAPTER TEN

TIDES AND RIVERS

Earth's oceans experience periodic rises and falls of water level. These are called tides. The moon causes tides. Newton's third law states that whenever two objects interact, they exert a force on each other. This is what happens when Earth and the moon interact. Even though Earth's gravitational force on the moon is much greater, the moon's gravitational force still has some effect on Earth.

LOW TIDE

TIDES CAUSED BY THE GRAVITATIONAL FORCE OF THE MOON

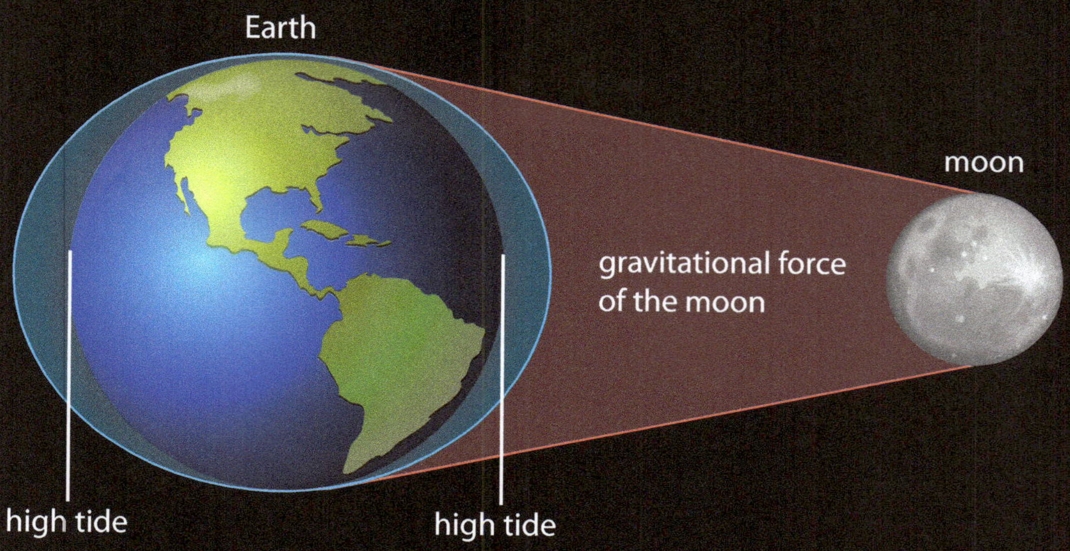

This picture shows how the moon's gravitational force causes the oceans closest to the moon and on the far side of Earth to bulge, creating high tide. The parts of the Earth not in this area experience low tide.

Gravity is also what causes rivers and streams to flow. Most rivers and streams begin high in the mountains as snow and ice. As the snow and ice melt, water runs down the mountains and creates rivers and streams. Gravity continues to pull the water down the slope of the land towards the lowest point, which is usually the ocean.

CHAPTER ELEVEN

MOTION IN SPORTS

Baseball pitchers usually put a little spin on a baseball when they throw it toward the batter. Because the ball spins as it moves through the air, the air flowing around the ball is pushed in different directions.

Newton's third law of motion states that, if the air is pushed down, the ball will rise. If the air is pushed up, the ball will sink toward the ground. Depending on what type of pitch they want to throw, the pitcher will spin the ball in a certain direction to produce the pitch they want.

The batter applies a force to the bat. When the bat touches the ball, the force is applied to the ball. The more force the batter applies to the bat, the farther the ball will go when it's hit.

In football, defensive linebackers use their bodies to try to stop the forward motion of their opponents. This is Newton's first law of motion in action!

Tulsa
24
Tulsa
65
GOLDEN
HURRICANE

CHAPTER TWELVE

MOTION AT THE AMUSEMENT PARK

Roller coasters use potential and kinetic energy to move. Potential energy is energy an object has because of its potential to move. A roller coaster gains potential energy when it's pulled up to the top of a hill. When the roller coaster goes down the hill, its potential energy changes to kinetic energy, or the energy of motion. Gravity causes the roller coaster to accelerate when it's going downhill and inertia keeps the ride moving as it goes back uphill.

When two bumper cars hit each other, each car exerts a force on the other. This is Newton's third law of motion in action.

When you're on rides at an amusement park, you experience different extremes of gravity. When a roller coaster or free-fall ride is going up, the pull of gravity presses you against the ride and it's hard for you to move. When the rides are going down, your body is no longer pressing against the ride and you feel weightless.

CHAPTER THIRTEEN

MAKING CARS SAFER

When you ride in a car, you and the car are traveling in the same direction at the same velocity. Imagine that, suddenly, the car stops. Even though the car has stopped moving, your body wants to continue moving due to inertia. If you don't have your seatbelt on, you could get hurt or even die.

The engineers who make the plans for cars are constantly trying to make cars safer. When a car crashes or stops suddenly, a seatbelt applies an opposing force to your body to prevent it from hitting something or being thrown from the car. A car airbag stops a person from hitting whatever's in front of them by changing their **momentum** and spreading out the force exerted upon them.

Crash test dummies, like the one in this car, help engineers understand how the human body reacts in different crash situations. In this photo, the dummy's head hits the airbag to prevent it from hitting the steering wheel.

20070

CHAPTER FOURTEEN

IT'S UNIVERSAL!

Scientists have learned a great deal about the nature of the universe since Newton published his laws of motion. They've learned that the universe is made up of microscopic particles and that even these incredibly small objects are in motion. In the early 1900s, Albert Einstein revised Newton's laws of motion to account for incredibly fast-moving objects, such as light, and incredibly large objects, such as stars.

Even though Newton's laws of motion have been updated in the nearly 350 years since they were first published, they remain a fundamental part of modern physics. Newton's laws of motion are universal because motion is universal. Motion is everywhere and it affects everything in our lives. When you think about the things in your life that have motion, imagining a world without motion is very strange.

GLOSSARY

acceleration (ihk-seh-luh-RAY-shuhn) The act or process of speeding up.

exert (ihg-ZUHRT) To put forth effort.

fluctuate (FLUHK-chuh-wayt) To change back and forth continually.

molecule (MAH-lih-kyool) The smallest possible amount of something that has all the characteristics of that thing.

momentum (moh-MEN-tuhm) The property that a moving object has because of its mass and its motion.

physicist (FIH-zuh-sihst) Someone who studies physics, or the science that deals with matter and energy and their interactions.

repetitive (rih-PEH-tuh-tiv) Happening again and again.

resistance (rih-ZIH-stuhns) An opposing or slowing force.

satellite (SAA-tuh-lyt) A spacecraft placed in orbit around Earth, a moon, or a planet to collect information or to communicate.

tendency (TEHN-duhn-see) A quality that makes something likely to happen or that makes someone likely to think or behave in a particular way.

theory (THEE-uh-ree) An idea suggested or presented as possibly true but not known or proven to be true.

velocity (vuh-LAA-suh-tee) Quickness of motion.

INDEX

PRIMARY SOURCE LIST

Page 7
Newton's own first edition copy of *Philosophiae Naturalis Principia Mathematica*. Sir Isaac Newton. 1687. Now kept by the Wren Library of Trinity College, Cambridge.

Page 21
Astronauts in microgravity. Photograph. March 10, 1997. Now kept by the NASA Image and Video Library.

Page 29
Crash testing at Ford Motor Co.'s Dearborn facility. Photograph. Jeff Kowalsky. March 10, 2014. Now kept by Bloomberg via Getty Images.

WEBSITES

Due to the changing nature of Internet links, PowerKids Press has developed an online list of websites related to the subject of this book. This site is updated regularly. Please use this link to access the list: www.powerkidslinks.com/sops/motion